LIGHT

AT

THE

TORN

HORIZON

LIGHT
AT
THE
TORN
HORIZON

PAUL MURRAY, OP

Published by the Word on Fire Institute, an imprint of
Word on Fire, Park Ridge, IL 60068
© Paul Murray, 2022
Printed in the United States of America

Cover design, typesetting, and interior art direction by
Rozann Lee, Michael Stevens, and Cassie Pease.

25 24 23 22   1 2 3 4

ISBN: 978-1-68578-025-8

Library of Congress Control Number: 2021922722

To Denis O'Brien
and
In memory of Dennis O'Driscoll

CONTENTS

III.

The Wound of Longing

IV.

Days and Hours

V.
Into the Light

A Reading

It opens like a river
in full spate, or like a window
with a gust of wind.
And it's as if an archangel
had entered the room. And everybody
has to stop what they're doing.
And the air is a river of words.
And all of a sudden you see
– and with a start –
that an archangel *has* entered,
and your heart is in your mouth.
And you feel you are drowning
in a river of divine words, and hear
yourself saying, over and over,
'How can this be?'

I.
The Shaken Branches

Weather

I know there will be other
days like this, other dawns
as bleak, other sudden
storms over the sea, other
driving winds as crazed
and untamed, pelting us
with their chill black rain.
But, most days,
there are moments also
of bold surprise in the
weather, when, if you wait,
as now, a gleam
strengthens at the torn
horizon, and light
– unimaginable light –
pours across the open
fields, brightening
the air above the distant
forest and the nearest
trees, shining clear
through the low, trembling
branches
dripping with rain.

Source

This is what my soul craves:
beauty of a kind that draws me
down to the root of my desire.
And you, Source of beauty,
responding to my need, have
planted signs for me to follow,
traces for me to track, a tide
of marvels at almost every step.
Yet even now distractions
hold me fast. I cannot reach
the depth to which I'm called.

O come, Spirit of God,
come to my aid, and breathe
upon my being with fresh
breath. Come, quicken
to new life the ancient sloth
of sense and spirit. Come
out of the glad music of a
mountain stream, or out
of a sudden storm, or a spring
breeze thick with orange and
apple blossom. O so inflame
these traces with your mark

it almost seems that, when
on slope and hill the wind shakes
out the scent of gorse, I can
breathe in your breath.

        O beauty's
hidden Source, take pity on
my blind dust, on my shadowed
heart's dumb ache.

Perspective

One day it's enough,
you feel, to view the world
　　through the common lens
of history, content
　　with no vision wider
than that of the obvious.

Next day, caught by
a tumult of longing, you search
　　among the straw and
chaff of things for the golden
　　corn of meaning.

Questions

1.

What improbable discord
of space and time
causes accident to dance,
the viruses
to blossom in the lungs,
the cruel slidings and collidings
of circumstance?

2.

Anyone who has looked,
really looked,
into the eyes of the innocent who suffer
will detect two things
being spoken.

First, with sadness:
There is no point
in seeking words
to match the measure of my pain
or anybody else's –
words are impossible.

But then, in striking contrast,
this question:

Can there not be found
on earth
words, human words,
to describe
what I am going through?

Naming

Quick now, before new fears
which would poison the blood
begin to spread, before grim
thoughts and images flood
the brain, name the darkest
threats, name the things
which hover and loom behind
the fears, confront them,
look them straight in the eye.
Lend them a myth, an image,
a story. Don't call them
threats, call them the bricks,
the stones of circumstance.
Catch them with a lightning
salvo of words even before
they hit. Hold them in a phrase
before they bruise.

Fate

Who knows what fate is –
                              It thrives
in its own realm,
with its own logic. It has no
language that can be deciphered,
no alphabet.
            If it had speech,
if it had words to speak,
they would be like stops of breath
or like arrows of light
                        in the dark,
or like darkness itself,
or like flowers
            rioting in the desert,
or like naked swords.

The Question

Can anyone find
a way backward through time?
No one can,
      no one
can breathe in last year's
apple-scented hours,
       no one
can re-live those moments
of unique, intense joy –
       a truth,
my mind tells me,
impossible to deny.
       How then
explain that, simply
by opening
a window
     and breathing in the night
air, heavy with scent
       of jasmine,
it is no longer night
but late morning
     and I am not
here, but walking
down a path fragrant
with herbs –
      around me, to the left

and right, hillside
and heath
      breathing
with life and freshness.

The Dying Poet

Who is the poet of doubt and hope
who believes, half-believes in miracles:
vision in the eyes of the blind,
canticles on the lips of the dumb?

                              I am that poet.

Who is the man, the singer, now
almost deaf and dumb, who longs
for earth music, music that remains
alive in the ear, alive in the blood?

                              I am that man.

Who is the fool, the madman, his last
hope hanging by a hair's breadth, who
puts the mouth of desire like a child
to the warm breast of the world?

                              I am that fool.

De la Musique

How to explain its
magic, this music of
deathless love and beauty,
   this Mozart?

It has a centre
of calm, but is not fixed,
not motionless
   or, if motionless,

then anchored
and steady, fixed
in one desire, a rumour
   of transcendence,

a burning,
a thing rooted in joy
and rising like a tall
   stamen

out of a dream
or like an invisible maypole
in the air, the swallows'
   plaything.

Ah, who can explain
this magic, this music
of deathless
    love and beauty?

Interrogation

Never easy to determine from where
the idea springs, or from which source
great art is born.
         From high above,
the Greeks would claim, from
rapture, from a blinding semi-divine
illumination.

No, the post-Freudians insist,
the opposite is the case, not from above
but from below,
         from the buried depths
of the psyche, from the fountain
of the dark unconscious.

Between these two, what to decide?

I confess I am torn. But one thing
is clear: should I attempt to interrogate
a work of art as to its origin,
         should I aim
grim arrows of inquiry
at a poem, a painting, a piece of music,

I could indeed squeeze out a few
answers in the end, but the risk might
well be fatal.
              The work itself, the thing
of beauty, will no doubt survive,
indifferent.

But that same beauty, or rather
my perception of its power,
worn down by the dogged pressure
of inquiry, may well
be found lying in pieces on my desk,

gasping for breath.

Survivors

    Perhaps in a crowd
he might be standing next to you, or she
might be your closest friend.
    No one knows
who they are. No one has the least idea
of the world from which they've come.
    If you knew their names,
if you knew the things they have endured,
you would be amazed.
    They look so poised, so much
at ease, so ordinary. No one knows
the tremendous secret they keep, how they
    hold in their hearts the tiredness
of earth's long history, the intimate, buried
memory of things unspeakable.

The Origins

How mysterious that leap,
 that primal urge of spirit –
  the desire to make

out of sound a first music
 and, with a strength
  of passion no less deep,

to stand for hours
 and hours at the rock face
  of a dark cave, giving

to the suddenness
 and chaos of things
  a form and colour.

Praise

And you, poet, what do you do? – I praise.
But the deadly, the monstrous things,
how can you accept them, bear them? – I praise.

Rainer Maria Rilke

When the deciphered years yield
no fruit of knowledge, and the only
harvest won is the wind's breath,
sing, poet, sing out your song.
When the tree of hallowed wisdom
tilts from its roots, and the purest
flame of truth is smothered,
half-smothered, by a smoke of lies,
sing, poet, sing out your song.
When bad news burns into
the brain – a scratched match flaring –
sing, poet, sing out your song.
When the shaken branches of
nightmare, and the worst of fears,
seem evergreen, un-withering,
sing, poet, sing out your song.
When even, at the end, your own
canticle appears as no more than
errant words on blurred pages,
sing, poet, sing out your song.

In the Forest

Late summer. The warm
green air of the forest
keeping us company
as we lay flat on the earth
looking up at the trees,
our unspoken
thoughts and dreams
bright and green
as the leaves and branches
hanging over our heads.

The Walk

Sleepless for an hour I got up
and, unmindful of wind or cold,
walked out into the night.
In less than a minute I stopped
and looked up. There were stars
behind stars behind stars.
How long I stood there I'm not
sure. I had no special thoughts.
A wiser man might know
how to read and interpret their
secret script. But I was content
all the same. The first drops
of rain on my hands and face,
the night wind rising,
and, holding their place, stars
behind stars behind stars.

II.
Look, There Is the Shore!

The Voice

Go back, if you can, to the beginning
– that's what I heard the voice whisper.
Your life, it's true, may not be glutted
with conceit, but it is still full of small
desires, and small in its desire. Go back
to the beginning. Return, if you can,
to the place your father would take you
when you were small, to the low-lying
wall that faces out to the open sea.

There, though at times your father might
say little or nothing, always
he was happy to let you babble on
about your child's games
and puzzles, talking and talking – until,
that is, the moment came
when you would both fall silent.

What would happen then? Impossible
to find the words even now to describe it,
how, in the long silence that followed,
such a wave of quiet would come over you,
it was as if, for the first time, you were
seeing and hearing all that lay before you:
the utterly still, utterly calm grandeur

of shore and mountain, sand and sea.
What could you do then but hold
your breath with wonder. You had no
words, no thoughts to help explain
what had occurred. You were too small
for thoughts. But something
changed all the same: a new, awakened
desire, a surge of joy
broke to the surface within you.

2.

What was it the voice whispered?
      Go back to the beginning,
return to the place
you would go to as a child. It is late
but not too late. The past is still open.
Even now you may recover your first dream.

Look, there is the shore and the sea
and the mountain.
      You are standing
next to your father beside the wall
that faces the sea.
      He is a hand's breadth away.

Mountain

It still towers over me,
the image of the granite
    mountain which, for years,
loomed above my childhood,
    and with majestic ease
stretched its long, grey
    boulders down to the sea.
Small parks and pathways,
    beloved hideaways, can
still be found round the corner
    of memory. These I can
easily seek out. But never
    the mountain. For that,
I have discovered, is no mere
    object of search or thought
or sentiment. Like a god
    on earth, before I could ever
seek out or choose
    my path, it had chosen me.

Wind

Rome, December 2020

Lifting out of the sea and rising
through the gaps and crevices
of memory, you can feel
against your skin the wind
of summer, its murmur and breath,
its warmth and touch
nearer to you now than ever.

The Flourishing Shrub

If the Kingdom of God had first been announced,
not in Palestine, but instead in a town, a place
near to the Mountains of Mourne, I feel sure
that the most likely symbol chosen would not
have been a dragnet, or a pearl, or a mustard seed,
and not even, perhaps, that most telling image
of life in the kingdom, the lilies of the field –
no, it would have been a plant, a shrub
so familiar to us we take it for granted, I mean
the gorse plant, that yellow-flowered, spiky,
evergreen bush that blossoms and thrives
all the year round in the valleys and on the hillsides
of Mourne, and flourishes even on the high,
rocky slopes of Slieve Binnian and Slieve Donard.

The Believers

So strong the memory, so radiant, it's hard
     not to credit the marvel of those
hot summer days spent at the beach.
     We were kids, and so naturally
the one dream in our heads was to leap
     into the water and, in among the waves,
make war and make fun for hours.
     But how could that be done?
With every step into the water
     we felt the waves' icy cold hand.
Why did it not stop us? What prompted us
     to believe we were nearer to
paradise than to our graves? Every day
     it was the same, the same cold sea,
the same wild screams of joy, the same
     unbelievable miracle of the waves.

Beginnings

Glimpses of a childhood
spent at the foot of The Mournes
more precious to me now
than hallowed works of art,
broken, half-broken memories
gleaming
like tiny shells buried in the rock.

A Winter Story

Is it possible that fear can spark
a blessing? Wakened out of sleep
by the sudden, chill harmony
of thunder and heartbeat, I could
feel terror up and down my spine.
But then something leaned towards me
out of the dark, and brushed
against my senses – a calming wave
of peace, a scent, a living warmth.
Never until that moment had I felt
so alive with fear and so loved.

Light Remembered

Miles inland from the sea,
we were on a path smelling of oak
and honeysuckle.
                    It was the tail-end
of an afternoon of warmth
and stillness, the whole day spent
wandering through the forest
at our ease.
                    My father
had been ill for years on and off.
                                    Could this
have been his last outing?
                                    I saw him stop
and look up. The light
in the sky, I remember, had turned
at that moment to honey-gold.

III.

The Wound of Longing

Noli me Tangere

The paradox of the believer's experience,
Augustine
nailed it in a sentence.

To the one who has doubts,
to Thomas Didymus,
the risen Lord declares
'Here, touch me!'

But to the one who believes and who seeks,
to Magdalen
who found Him in the garden,
Christ says
'Do not touch me!'

Prayer

It took me many years
to realize a simple truth.
What matters most
is not the felt presence
of God, nor is it some
ecstatic grace of rapture.
It is instead the lost
untamed desire, the beggar's
ache, the wound
of longing in the heart.

Divine Hide and Seek

This is a tiresome game!

Blessed Henry Suso

Truly you are a hidden God.
For days, for weeks on end,
I have watched for you in prayer,
I have kept vigil. But hour
to hour, day to day, you remain
distant, unspeaking. You keep
faith with the game.
Undeflected, and with a child's
utterly calm, purposeful intensity,
you remain in hiding. I can
find you nowhere. I am so lost
in a labyrinth of shadows,
and so blind to your radiance,
it is as if I am still holding my hands
over my eyes, and still counting.

O Merciful One

When without hope, without aim,
we find ourselves turning and turning
on the outermost rim
of the circumference of our own lives –

When our hearts are cold, our minds
no longer open to the conviction
of the unseen
or to the sources of that conviction –

When words which were fiery
once, electrifying the mind and heart,
now seem but a mimicry of
flame, a dazzle of frozen sparks,

burn us with your fire of truth,
with your flame of love.

In the Future

Should it happen
that my thoughts of you,
of your fire
    and of your beauty,
find themselves trapped
in a predictable,
    dull pattern of
words, and start to lose
all depth, all freshness,
    help me,
O living Word, to teach
those thoughts
    that need to die
how to die, and those
dead words how to live.

Words of the Mystics

Words so luminous they startle the mind
    with un-shadowed
meaning, leaving images
    that remain
etched in the mind for years.
    Words of rare and naked candour.

Transfigured words, words risking
    exposure to both storm and stillness,
to quick, sudden
    bonfires of emotion, and to the most
cold,
    most silent caverns of thought.

Words like seeds buried
    in the womb of the earth. Words,
which long before
    they came to birth on the page,
before they flourished
    in our minds, had first been broken.

Lines for the Afflicted

1.

Closer than you can imagine,
the world on the other side
of the senses. Go back there,
learn to breathe deep with
new lungs, with new hope,
let the wounded years cast off
their yoke. Let healing start.

2.

No one knows what you feel.
No one knows what dragged you
from your dreams, from hillsides,
rivers, fountains, friendship,
laughter. No one understands,
no one knows what fresh fear
takes hold when the black wind
rises, and new spears of terror
stand in your veins, and thoughts,
like startled birds turned back
against the wind, begin to wheel
and scatter. No one knows
the appalling dread at the heel
of a half-turn in the road,
when you find you are no longer

there but are walking instead
in the valley of desolation.

3.
Maybe an angel,
a dove of light,
an unimaginable
angel whose heart
is human, and can
break, might find
the necessary words,
but I cannot.
My stricken
thoughts and words
are too controlled,
benign,
not flayed enough.

Impossible Words

Faltering, necessary words,
words longing to be more than words,
longing to be more like silence
or like action.

Words in the face of unspeakable beauty,
of unspeakable anguish,
words of shame and hope
blushing at themselves.

IV.
Days and Hours

The Choice

Well, here I am out early
in the morning, and as Auden
would say, 'in solitude for company.'

It's 6 a.m., and I've just
returned from a short, meditative
trek around the block.
                              Outside,
the yellow lamps
are still lighting, and the streets
are wet after the rain.

Overhead, and all around,
the bowl of the sky is dark,
dark for miles and miles.

But it's bright here
this morning under these lamps.

Who would ever
choose – given the choice –
to live anywhere else?

The Green Man

His eyes, his lips
and brow are circled
by vines, leaf-thick
and apple-green.
He has a smile like
no other. Though
haloed by leaves
and by the shadows
of leaves, his is a
countenance of light.
His message is one
of rebirth. In his
eyes the last cold
gaze of winter dies
and green wheat
waves and billows.

He is a happy seer,
a minor prophet
dazed and amazed
at his own revealing.
His songs
are those of nesting
birds and of spring
storms. His thoughts
are zones of joy.

But he is not tame.
He is too brazen
to be tame, his
feelings bold
and unpredictable
as the wind.
With crude hands
he holds intercourse
with roots of trees
and stones,
and with his eyes
he laughs and weeps
with fountains and
rivers at their source.

Devoted as a slave
to the taste and
shimmer of things,
he loves to wade
in the shallows.
He has no love for
the heights or for
the depths. And yet
there is a secret
he keeps hidden,
even from himself:

he is in love with
death as much as
life, the happy,
unhappy poet
of all that passes.

The Seeker

I had not spared myself.
I had been bold in my endeavour.
In the great search for wisdom
I had travelled near and far,
and never tired of seeking out
the celebrated names.
                    But one day
one line in one work
stopped me in my tracks.
How I blushed, ear to ear,
as it sang into my heart:
'Stand still, and do not waver
from your emptiness!'

On Emptiness

It may make you shudder for
a moment when, out
of nowhere, you experience,
in the midst of life's clutter
and haste, a void in the
heart, a shock like
that of stepping off a footpath
and missing your step.
But there's no need to panic
or be afraid. Listen again
to the calm teaching of Meister
Eckhart: *Stand still. Do not*
waver from your emptiness.

To the Hidden God

I cannot say always,
I cannot even say often,
but sometimes I have felt your close regard,
You
at the eye of the storm,
You, the single eye,
the calm
that fills my whole being with light.

The Hours

They belong to neither time
nor space, the unknown,
undated hours of the future.
Theirs is a world
without fear, without pain
– unimaginable – and yet
they are as real
as the hours of the past
– or almost. In their world
no light flames, no vision,
yet something leans
towards them all the same.
If they had lungs, they would
be holding their breath.

The Silence

For you
there is no hiding, no disguise
that works,
no matter how much you try
to look disinterested,
or turn
your face away.

The memory remains,
the hurt.
It fills your eyes like tears.

You never
bring up the past,
or speak of the pain itself, as if
at the edge of pain
there is no more pain to speak of.

Instead,
each day you bring to the beauty
of the day
your weariness.

You bring it as if to an altar
and lay it down there
in silence.

The Visionaries of Non-Violence

At the hour of threat, who comes
nearer to the edge
      than these warriors of peace?

Who lives closer
      to the gap
between dream and catastrophe?

         If not these men,
these women, who are the true
antagonists of evil,
      the real warriors of the spirit?

Who manifests more
      courage in the fight,
more daring?
      Who takes the greater risk?

         The only shield
they possess, their only armor,
an impossible,
      possible dream.

Their hands and feet,
    their blood and speech, un-barred
and un-armed.

Who stands
      nearer to the edge,
         closer to the gap
between dream and catastrophe?

Wound

No matter if the heart
has hardened. There is still
time to recover
and heal, time for the arrow
of beauty to pierce
through to the deepest wound.
It is a new day.
Look up. Yellow light is already
flooding the sky.

The Failed Canticle

I threw the pages into the fire
and watched them turn to smoke.
    I was disappointed. I had hoped
to compose a song, a prayer,
a canticle of praise. But even
    before I threw the pages
into the flames, the prayer itself
had turned to ashes in my mouth.
    Ah, how miserable, how hollow
the words sounded in my ears!
But as I watched the smoke rising
    I thought of that other fire,
the immanent, invisible fire of God
which burns both fierce and
    gentle, and of how, in that flame,
even the poorest prayer survives,
and rises in the air, not like
    doomed smoke, but like a lifting
cloud of incense, trembling
words aflame with love and hope.

On Hayling Island

Late July 1966

Memory, whittled down
to its core, can grow lean
and lacklustre,
drear and granite grey.
But on the island
that morning,
as I remember it now,
under the sullen air, under
the drifts of rain,
one face alone –
her face –
caught and held the sun.

Legacy

If only as a scar
        etched
on time's shoulder, something
always remains
            of the seer's
or the prophet's teaching:
                a rare
luminous anecdote,
for example, or a remembered
saying,
    or a few lines
from an otherwise long-forgotten
psalm,
    or a fragment
of irascible verse,
            four or five
leathery stanzas of complaint,
gnarled and spiky.

Cézanne

No artist can tell for sure
if, on the other side of risk,
what awaits is success
or failure. And fear of failure
can get into the bones
of the finest painters,
into the hands,
and into the palette itself.

But Cézanne, standing out
in the open, stared down
that fear on an average day.
Reckless as a gambler, but
shrewd and watchful as a fox,
no fear of failure ever
stopped him from throwing
his whole being on a colour.

Day to Day

The heart has its thickets
and hedgerows, its rugged peaks
    and slippery paths. One day
I am not afraid to step out
    into the brightest clearings,
to stand there drinking in the light,
    the stillness. But, next
day, hit by a storm or by a hurt
    that strikes from within,
the blood halts in my veins
    and I step back into shadow.

That stepping back is never
wise. If only I could learn the hard
    lesson fear wants to hide
from me, the paradox that if I stand
    my ground and lean
into the hurt, a new, irrepressible
    jet of light and freshness
will begin to rise,
    and, out of the pit of fear,
out of the heart of the storm,
    a new fountain of courage.

Finishing a Poem

How to describe the relief,
the delight?
It's as if you had been
striking a match
that would not catch,
but then suddenly
it flares – the surprise,
after hours of failure,
at finding a music,
a rhythm
native to your tongue,
when words
and images combine
to achieve
unexpected vision.

Days and Hours

There's no way to explain them
or contain them, no way to hold
them in your grasp,
those radiant days, radiant hours,
when the mind is filled with
a bee swarm of ideas
and the heart lifts in a dolphin's
arc of sheer delight.
                    Ask the young
man or woman in love,
ask the artist, poet, painter,
sculptor –
they will all tell you the same.

Rilke's Imperative

Along the tallest bark
and in the veins of trees
it runs, among the
rustling corn and in the jade
shallows, in the sloe
thorn and in the wild rose
it calls and calls –
You must change your life.

The Animals' Messiah

The whole of creation has been groaning
in one great act of travail,
and we too groan inwardly as we await
the redemption of our bodies.

Romans 8:22–23

Out in the wild they are all waiting,
the mountain hares, the feral goats,
the deer, the stoats, the white-tailed
eagles, the badgers, the grey squirrels.
How much longer must they wait?
When will redemption finally come
to bird and beast, to fowl and fish?

On the marvel that is the earth,
in the beauty of ocean and desert,
of forest and tundra, in the skies
and in the fields of wonder,
they remain innocent prey to one another.
Everywhere, the same carnage,
the same law beating in the blood:
murder or starve, kill or be killed.

Out in the wild they are all waiting.

Diogenes of Dublin

He inhabited no jar or tub on the street like Diogenes
but he did choose to live rough like the Greek, carrying
around with him all he possessed in two loaded
knapsacks. A down-and-out with a broken cheek, he could
be meek on occasion, even friendly, but was mostly
cantankerous. A thought-possessed tramp, a street
thinker, he was light years ahead of the new atheists, his
bold theological stance summed up in one phrase: 'I don't
believe in the Quare Fella, the point is he doesn't
intervene!' He bore the scars of battles, mostly with other
men on the street but sometimes battles too with the
police. These scars he wore like medals. But one November
night he phoned and for the first time whispered in a
broken voice, 'I need help.' This time he had been beaten
badly, his face and hands a mess of blood. 'Where will I
meet you?' I asked. 'Meet me,' he replied, and I could hear
at once the stoic, undefeated grin in his voice, 'Meet me at
the front door of Massey's Funeral Parlour!'

The Theatre of Joy

There is a category of genius
which has not yet found a name.

Let imagination take a bow
and the dance of words
and redemptive music.

Call back for an encore
the angels of light and laughter.
Rise up to applaud them.

Paradise is here on the bare stage.
Disillusion be damned.

Humour will save the world.

Canticle in Praise of Punctuation

Most high, omnipotent, and good Lord,
unseen, unknown Author and inspirer
  of every word that dances on the page
in front of us, and leaps in our blood,
  and of every dot and comma that we read
in the grammar of the Book of Life;
  Hidden Poet, invisible planner of beauty
from before the beginning, you are
  praised and honoured in all your creatures
and in all the marvellous features of your
  creation. But, in the grammar of our lives,
among the great and small features
  of Punctuation, you are especially known
to us in the presence of your tiny servant,
  our humble sister, the Comma.

O Maker of all good things, it is amazing
  to us that you should so attend
to the page on which we shape our lives
  as to give us the Comma.
She, though she may appear
  the least of all to the eye of the reader,
has already found her place
  in the kingdom of the sentence.
What, then, does she care if, line by line,
  she goes unnoticed among the important

nouns and verbs and adjectives? Her task,
    though small, is sharp and beautiful.

    O Word, utterly present, utterly hidden,
we also praise you and give you honour
    for our noble brother, the Colon.
He, though he stands at the inner gate
    of the sentence, like a sign of division,
is grammar's gentleman. He is the quiet
    bond, the hinge that swings
between two linked but separate worlds.

    O Master of surprise,
author of un-covenanted grace, you are also
    vividly recalled for us in that wild
and uncontrollable sibling of ours,
    that brash improviser
of customs and rules, that bold disrupter
    of lives and of lines,
the Colon's youngest brother – the Dash!

And, not to be confused with her
    plain brother, the Colon,
or with her humble sister, the Comma,
    we praise you, Lord, and we thank you
for that most exquisite sign
    of your presence among us,
the Semi-Colon. Even in mid-sentence,

among the week-day hassle
of words and meanings, her image
    on the page always denotes a pause,
a tiny Sabbath, and a time to breathe.

    O invisible Flame, Word of hidden
fire, we thank you also for that brilliancy
    which falls like lightning on the page,
     that sharp and handsome sign of certitude,
     that sword of truth, our brother,
your servant, the Exclamation Mark!

    And no less vital for our
lives and words, but in a form which
    stops and spirals on its stem,
that grace of doubt and hesitation,
    that stubborn thing, the honest
shape of the Question Mark.

And, always in flight, hovering
    above our lives and lines
like infinitesimal birds, or like tiny bees,
    we thank you for our twin-sisters,
the Inverted Commas. You have
    made them, above all other signs,
the connoisseurs of citation, the bearers
    of echoes and images
from worlds outside the sentence,

the minute seers of the
honey of distant voices and colours,
   the celebrants of difference.

   O Beginning and End of all things,
you are worthy of all praise and all honour
   and so we thank you even for
that sign which stands at the bright margin
   where the sentence ends,
that dot of grace, that necessary thorn
   in the flesh of the grammar of our lives,
that minor prophet of our own demise,
   our tiny brother – the Full Stop.

V.

Into the Light

Hope Against Hope

When will it come,
will it ever come,
the great tide of blessing
we were promised,
peace flowing like a river
upon Jerusalem?

I say to myself, what
I say to others:
be attentive and wait.
Already, perhaps,
out of the darkest hollows
and crevices

of night, tiny
streams high up on the
mountains,
are beginning to gather
force. And, closer
than you can imagine,

a river
you have never seen
or known is flowing clear,
flowing deep
and clear into the light of
morning.

Words for Siún

The rain steadying somewhat,
you step out from the half-lights
and shadows

         and lift your hand
to wave.

       That lone, simple gesture,
why does it burn

         so strong?
Now, even now, you are turning
your gaze

       to where I'm standing
on the still-wet shore

         of stopped time.

The Awakening

Among the rags
and remnants
of an ordinary day,
the discovery
of a radiance
no longer hidden,
a gathered light
shining
from things taken
for granted
over many years,
the piercing
shock at being
so completely
blind
to what was so near
and so obvious.

To a Friend Dying

It is still dark, and darkness
surrounds you, but do not be afraid.
        Now is the moment of grace.
The tide of love, which all your life
        has flowed out secretly
to you from God, begins now
        to turn back to its source.
Now, as your spirit fails, you can
        with your last breath
breathe deep and feel another's
        breath inhale and breathe
within your breath. His life is yours
        and light shines through you
on all that surrounds you,
        and the whole heart watches over
what is happening now.

Seeing the Waterfall

Invisible God,
when I first saw that curtain of light
and freshness, that bright
explosion of water
over rock,
I felt for a moment I had caught
a glimpse of you
– unimaginable thought! –
breaking free
from one of your hiding places.

Address to the Lions

When those who love God try to talk
about him, their words are
blind lions
looking for springs in the desert.

Léon Bloy

A statement as honest
as it is compelling,
but, trust me, a day will
come when at last
the wind will begin to lift
and the sky to darken,
and rain, torrents of rain,
will pelt down
on this desert of yours,
and immeasurable, tiny
drops of cold light
will leap and dance
on the sand, and you will
feel water splashing
over your tired limbs
and blind eyes, and you
will know at last
that the long drought
has passed, and that,

already, fresh springs are
rising within you, and
that never again will
hope fade like a skein
of low cloud
passing over the sand.

At the Edge

Something came and went
at yesterday's full tide, a light over the water,
a radiance in the air
so strong
it seemed almost a miracle.

Soon, all that was left was a blur
at the edge of vision,
a spent nimbus,
a gleam so far out in the distance
no eye could see it.

But then, the tide turned.

Night Song

A black cloud
balances its soul
against the moon.

Close by, on hazel
shrub and hawthorn,
night dew falls.

There is not
the least breath
of wind.

An hour more still,
more illumined,
I have never known.

Five Disguises of the Soul

Only about my soul I know nothing.

Marin Sorescu

1.

Gesture

The way that young woman who, just now
is standing in the doorway, turns her head
sideways, and with such extraordinary grace,
brings at once to mind the young mother
in Caravaggio's Pilgrim Painting, her gesture
as quick and unaffected as it is compelling.

Who can understand the impact of beauty?
When it strikes, when it pierces deep,
it awakens the senses. But, in the quickness
of the moment, present also is a flame
of spirit, a beauty from within which hides
in every gesture and in every turning glance.

2.
Path

A path is like the soul. It is something
that leads you forward. You take
steps, you walk, you move
in a direction, but the force behind
the steps, the impetus which gets you
moving, is from a source of which,
at times, you may be wholly unaware.

3.
Conscience

Quite often he can appear as a prophet,
an outright stranger. But, when he arrives,
it's from no zone,

            no realm of spirit
other than your own.

                See, how relaxed
he looks! He is serene. He doesn't need
to say a word, much less hold up a mirror.
But glance at him,

            even for a second,
and, in his gaze, you will catch a luminous
signal of recognition.

You may be startled, at first,

                  but stand your ground

and hold steady.

Soon behind his eyes you will discover

there is another,

             a further radiance.

He is nearer to you now than your own

breath. He is not your enemy.

4.

Music

What, on occasion, can both

betray and hide the soul is not

the music itself, and not even

the words of the song, but rather

the gap, the space between

the words, the sudden quiet, the

stillness when the music stops.

5.

Wave

To make a start, take this thought, this word
of wisdom from Pasternak. It comes straight
from the soul: 'Everything
in the world must excel itself to be itself.'
So, be bold. Take whatever it is
that propels you beyond what seems possible
but still anchors you in the here and now.
Take the awakening of desire, the calling
to new and fresh purpose.
Take the wave of tenderness that
overwhelms you when you fall in love,
the feeling of being lifted out of yourself,
and living on breaths of air.
Take the jolt to the heart, the sweet
catastrophe love demands, the painful joy
of losing and finding self.
Take the courage of being able to confront
head on the trammels and trials of life
and yet hold fast to hope. Take the dream
that was weighed down by chains
but is now bearing impossible/possible
wings.
            'Everything
in the world must excel itself to be itself.'

Green Music

Foolish to think it, I know,
but sometimes after rain
when I walk out into the open
I imagine I hear not only
the small birds' antiphon
sounding more clear
than ever, but also the music
of the tongues of stones
washed clean, and the music,
everywhere I look or turn,
of the singing greenness
of trees and tall grasses.

The Lost Time

They usually say lost time cannot be recovered. But what is impossible for you who can do everything? Recover, my God, the lost time by giving me grace in the present . . . for if you want to, you can do so.

St Teresa of Avila

Bear with me, Lord, it takes
time to absorb the radiance
of such a thought, the idea
that you can win back
time lost, and turn the feeling
of remorse into gratitude,
and that of fear into praise.
But why should I doubt
your power? Time and time
again, you have changed
the dark poem of winter
into spring, and turned ice
into fire, and sent the sap
of hope rising through
wearied stems and tendrils
of lost dreams.

A single wish
of yours, a breath
like thunder, was it not enough
to set the stunned universe
spinning on its axis? Why
should I doubt your power?

Call

Find it, the path that's still
wide open
to a world of unimaginable
joy and fulness –
      to the sheer pleasure
a mountain stream takes
in finding its form, or a birch tree
or a waterfall.
      Discover, re-discover
the path that leads
to freedom, it is still yours.
         Look up,
just ahead of you and still
within reach, birds of happiness
are flying and flurrying.

Paradise

It's not every day
you find yourself walking in Paradise
    with Virgil.
Both of us, I'd say, were amazed
    at our good fortune.
He, the unbaptized, and me,
    the undistinguished,
minor poet who had somehow
    skipped Purgatory.
There were no fires
    anywhere to be seen.
The only flames were colours
    in the mosaic floor
and in the light that shone
    through all the windows.
Turning to him, I said: What was it
    opened for you the door
to Paradise? Was it a determined
    longing for what is true
and good? Was it a baptism of desire?
    I really have no idea, he said,
the only virtue I've known, over
    the years, has been the long
patience of waiting for illumined
    words to burn clear.

And you, he asked, turning
 in my direction, how did you
get here? I was stumped. I searched
 my brain for answers. Then
it came – how could I have
 forgotten? Once, back on earth
I wrote a poem called *Paradise*.
 It was a game, a dance
of words, no more, but the words
 made all this happen,
and here we are. As I spoke, the dream
 itself was fading, but I had
time to tell him how the poem
 begins: *It's not every day*
you find yourself walking in Paradise
 with Virgil.

Words

Almost nothing in human history
more momentous than the moment
when the first ecstatic words,
the first miracles of sound were breathed
into the air. How astonishing
they must have seemed to themselves
at that moment, our rugged
ancestors – one word after another
tumbling from their lips! And, to this
day, that hunger has never
ceased, that thirst for sound, for words.
It's there in every child and every poet –
lips seeking words like fresh water.

Afterword

1.

What does a poem
    bring in the end
if not a new radiance
    of perception,

unguarded words

lifting common speech
    from the rubble
of dead forms
    and tired phrases.

2.

What does a poem
    bring in the end
if not a temporary
    pause between tasks,

stolen time

at ease with either
    the formal magic of rhyme
or the music and freedom
    of a rugged idiom.

3.

What does a poem
    bring in the end
if not news
    from the sunken life,

memory restored

from a buried world
    of history and vision,
images from a lost
    archipelago of dreams.